ADVENTURES IN COMPASSION

Celebrating a History of Compassion.

Black History Month 2014

Rahbin Shyne

In memory of Nelson Mandela.

Contents

FOREWORD 6

COMPASSION IN ACTION 1

DAY 1: ACKNOWLEDGE A CHILD 6

DAY 2: RAISE MONEY FOR CHARITY EVERY TIME
YOU SEARCH ONLINE 8

DAY 3: ACKNOWLEDGE SOMEONE YOU KNOW 11

DAY 4: GIVE YOUR CHANGE TO CHARITY 13

DAY 5: LISTEN TO SOMEONE 16

DAY 6: CLEAN SOMETHING 18

DAY 7: SMILE 20

DAY 8 GIVE AWAY ONE DOLLAR 22

DAY 9 THANK THOSE WHO SERVE 25

DAY 10 EXPRESS THANKS 27

DAY 11 ACKNOWLEDGE A STRANGER 29

DAY 12 GIVE AWAY A BOOK, MUSIC OR ART 31

DAY 13 SHARE A TALENT 33

DAY 14 DONATE SOMETHING TO CHARITY 35

DAY 15 EXPRESS YOUR GRATITUDE 38

DAY 16 WATCH YOUR WORDS 40

DAY 17 LOVE YOU 42

DAY 18 GIVE 10 MINUTES 44

DAY 19 SAY "I LOVE YOU." 46

DAY 20 PLAY ONLINE GAMES, GENERATE
DONATIONS 48

DAY 21   DO SOMETHING FOR THE PLANET 51

DAY 22   COMPASSIONATE TOUCH HEALS..........................53

DAY 23   MAKE A REQUEST...55

DAY 24   LET LAUGHTER HEAL.......................................57

DAY 25   FORGIVE SOMEONE..59

DAY 26   GIVE SOMETHING TO SOMEONE 61

DAY 27 CALCULATE YOUR GLOBAL FOOTPRINT 64

DAY 28 CREATE A BETTER WORLD 66

DAY 29   REPEAT YOUR FAVORITE COMPASSIONATE
ACT 68

DAY 30   INSPIRE COMPASSION.......................................70

*"Religion without humanity is very poor
human stuff."
—Sojourner Truth*

FOREWORD

*"Our human compassion binds us the one
to the other - not in pity or patronizingly,
but as human beings who have learnt how
to turn our common suffering into hope for
the future."*
- Nelson Mandela

I love the above quote. It reminds us that simple acts of
kindness can inspire significant change. Every day we
can make a difference in someone's life, no matter how
small the act may seem.

This particular edition of the Compassion Series
highlights historic African-Americans and our rich
history of compassion. We adopt friends into our families
as "cousin", "brother" "sister" and "aunt." We love to
feed anyone and everyone visiting our homes. Many of us
fondly remember a neighborhood "mama" where kids
and adults alike could eat, sleep, play and learn; with
motherly advice and motherly discipline freely given.
My mother was my neighborhood's "mama" and I remain
inspired by the depth of her compassion.

I remember, as a child growing up in Tulare, CA, hearing
our church choir sing "I Want to Be More like Jesus."
Sister Woods' petite form would soothingly sing "I want
to be more like Jesus, every day," and the choir would
follow with "every hour of the day!" Jesus fed the
hungry, clothed the poor, prayed for the masses and
listened, with full attention, to everyone with whom He

spoke. Most importantly, He loved –from the smallest to the greatest.

The values held by a great majority of African-Americans centers around our daily efforts to emulate the principles taught by Jesus. We are not perfect nor are our heroes. But this book is not about being perfect. It is about seeking that which makes our human lives better; that which enriches humanity. That is what our history of compassion has always encouraged.

This is what guides my practice as a physician. Friends and family often ask me why I choose to work in a hospital setting, with its sleepless nights, instead of 9am-5pm in a clinic. Over time, I came to realize it was the opportunity to be a source of calm for families during a time of stress and fear. I have always gravitated to the practice of medicine in high-intensity, emotionally charged areas. When a child is hospitalized, I strive to be the face of compassion for that family. If like me, you strive to better our communities and world, to be the face of compassion, this book is for you.

My prescription for Black History Month in 2014 is 30 days of compassionate action. I am confident that you will love, recommend and share Celebrating a History of Compassion with friends and family, alike.

So get to it. Doctor's orders!

Donna C. Carey, MD
Pediatrician
President, Sinkler Miller Medical Association
Women's Ministry Leader, True Vine Ministries, Oakland, CA

COMPASSION IN ACTION

*"If you find it in your heart to care for
somebody else, you will have succeeded."*
– Maya Angelou

The Adventure

I think it is fair to say that the history of Negroes, of
Blacks, of African-Americans is a history of compassion
in action. From Frederick Douglas to Martin Luther
King; from Sojourner Truth to Shirley Chisholm, we
recognize that compassion is not a feeling. It is not
sympathy. Compassion is an act that validates and honors
the humanity of another. Someone else's life is better off
because we took the time to care.

What better way to participate in Black History Month
than through living the values embodied in the men and
women commemorated?

All are invited to participate in February 2014's
Adventure in Compassion, Celebrating a History of
Compassion. Each day, February 1st to March 2nd,
complete the day's designated action of compassion. This
month of compassionate action will bring more love and
generosity to our homes, neighborhoods and world. Don't
miss this opportunity to celebrate history by making it.

This limited edition compilation of historic figures will
be available from January 1st to March 15th only.

The Inspiration

The entire world needs a boost, not just one community, sub-group or color. Each title in The Compassion Series can be completed by anyone and everyone, regardless of race, sex, gender, income or age. However, two things led me to create an edition aligned with Black History Month.

The first is Nelson Mandela's recent passing. He was inspired by the success of the nonviolent civil rights movement here in America which, in turn, was inspired by the success of Mahatma Gandhi. Mandela's commitment to a more humane system of government in South Africa is legendary.

When offered a conditional release after serving two decades in prison, he refused to compromise his position. He made clear he was unwilling to be singled out from those who struggled alongside him for special release. His commitment was not for his own sake, but for his fellow countrymen. He was clear about it. In the end he became South Africa's first Black President and was awarded the Nobel Peace Prize along with F.W. de Klerk, the last president under the then defunct apartheid system. If that does not exemplify compassion, I don't know what would.

The second inspiration is a home grown, powerhouse couple committed to bettering Oakland through compassion. Pastor Zachary Carey has spent three years building Stand Against Violence Everywhere (SAVE) an organization dedicated to reducing the epidemic of gun violence destroying urban communities. Dr. Donna C. Carey is committed to providing quality healthcare in underserved communities to ensure youth thrive rather than diabetes, stress and heart disease. They are working toward the same outcomes embodied in the budding Compassion Movement—safer, healthier communities where everyone thrives.

This month we give tribute to the many African-American heroes and heroines, past and present, who have bettered our world. We honor them by doing our part in creating safer, healthier communities. This month we honor a history of compassion with our own compassionate actions.

We start on February 1st and end on March 2nd in 2014. Register your church, workplace, organization or family at ShyneEveryDay.com. If just 34,000 people join in and complete each day's action, we'll have a month of one million compassionate acts to show for it.

Except for giving away a dollar and giving away a favorite book, you can complete the 30 actions without taxing your personal resources. This adventure only costs stepping outside your comfort zone once or twice.

Why 30 Days?

After thirty days, compassion becomes a habit not easily dropped. The first time I completed one of the Adventures in Compassion, I found myself experiencing more joy and love in the ordinary moments of life. The heart and soul grows exponentially with each day's act of compassion.

You don't have to do all thirty days. Even if you only take the actions for a week or two, benefits will flow to yourself and others. But, in my humble opinion, if Nelson

Mandela could spend 27 years in prison to better his country, I don't think taking a few minutes to complete one compassionate action a day for 30 days is asking too much.

I guarantee that if you commit to the thirty days, you will experience a profound sense of love, connection and an expansion in your experience of personal power. Yes, I said, guaranteed. (By the way, gyms could guarantee weight loss if you actually work out three times a week and adjust your diet accordingly. So, yes, I guarantee a profound shift *if* you complete the entire adventure.)

And there's a prize

A handful of readers turned compassion adventurers will earn the lofty title "Grandmaster of Compassion" by completing each day's challenge without skipping a beat. To those of you who complete all thirty actions on the very first go-round, Kudos! Your prize is a title. There will be a badge of honor for you to download or post at ShyneEveryDay.com beginning March 1st. The true prize, of course, is the expansion of your heart.

Honor and celebrate a rich history of compassion by living it today. Like love, this game is more fun when shared. Invite friends, family, coworkers, church members, book club, meet-up group, knitting circle or neighbors to propel you forward with a little friendly competition.

Need a fundraiser?
Get all the members in your group, church, charity or workplace to accept pledges from friends, family and

coworkers for each day's completed action. Try 10cents/day or $1 for each day's act of compassion. That will net $3 or $30 per pledge at month's end. Have some fun, spread some love and raise some cash for a cause that nurtures your community.

It's a love thing

Love is the foundation of compassionate action. Love appears wherever and whenever we give it a space to show up, and stays as long as we court its presence. It's not a feeling. It's doesn't dwell in a fixed state. It can't be copyrighted, patented, re-engineered, rationed, bottled or monopolized. It flows out of us and into us. The more love we make and give away, the more light we have for ourselves. Share your love. Share your light. Shyne Every Day.

"Life's most persistent and urgent
question is 'What are you doing for
others?"
– Martin Luther King, Jr.
Civil Rights Activist

DAY 1: ACKNOWLEDGE A CHILD

"It is easier to build strong children, than repair broken men."
– Frederick Douglass
Abolitionist, Author

Today's Adventure

Tell a young person a unique way they are wonderful and precious.

Compassion in Action

Each child is a unique gift, unwrapped a little more each day through their interactions with others and their environment.

The unwrapping happens when we share words of affirmation. Every time we affirm or pronounce what is unique and blessed about them, children grow a little stronger. Our children need that extra strength, that extra assurance.

If your day will not take you into the company of a young person, think about an underage sibling, cousin, nephew, niece, or other young person you can call just to say hello and hear what they have to say. You might spark a conversation that wouldn't happen otherwise.

Mastering Compassion

Most of us know at least one child that can truly try our patience. Show your compassion by understanding this young person will benefit by positive affirmation of his or her better qualities to balance the negative reactions his or her bad behavior inspires. At the moment you most want to correct, admonish or otherwise react to this child, find something positive to say and say it.

Keeping Score

Who did you acknowledge?

What did you say?

What did you notice about you, the child or what happened next?

If you did not complete it, what got in the way?

"My mother never gave up on me. I messed up in school so much they were sending me home, but my mother sent me right back."
– Denzel Washington
Actor, Academy Award Winner

DAY 2: RAISE MONEY FOR CHARITY EVERY TIME YOU SEARCH ONLINE

*"If you are going to achieve excellence in
big things, you develop the habit in little
matters. Excellence is not an exception, it
is a prevailing attitude."*
- Colin Powell
U. S. Secretary of State

Today's Action

Let your internet searches generate donations to charity.

Compassion in Action

With information at our fingertips, we search out answers to any question that crosses our mind and holds our attention longer than ten seconds. Today, searching for answers earns money for charities. You get to be compassionate on someone else's ½ cents.

EcoSearch.org and SearchKindly.org are two of many. These and similar sites, partner with major search engines to complete your web searches. Then they donate all or a portion of the profits from advertising revenue. In the case of EcoSearch.org, they donate 100% of their profits to charities that promote a healthier environment. That's not 100% of revenue, so they still pay staff and other costs to run the business. However, if you're searching anyway, why not do so with a company that gives something back. Your search engine choice is a chance to donate someone else's money. See how easy this is!

The two I've listed are powered by Google. You'll get exactly the same search results as with Google.

If you prefer Yahoo's algorithms, use GoodSearch.org. Plus, GoodSearch.org lets you choose from over 100,000 different charities. Choose huge and national or small and local. GoodSearch.org asks that you create a login or link to your Facebook account before selecting a charity or cause. If you find that GoodSearch.org includes a favorite charity, why not make them your homepage and give to a cause you care about every time you surf? If everyone in your church, group or club does the same; your favorite charity gets a windfall without you doing anything different.

Whichever you choose, today's searching makes a difference. If you have no reason to use a search engine today, complete tomorrow's activity two days in a row. You can still use one of these do-good engines next time you surf.

Why not make Ecosearch.org, SearchKindly.org, GoodSearch.org or another charitable browser your homepage, using it for all your searches over the next month, year or from now on?

While your searches may only generate pennies a day, your pennies plus the pennies of a million others is still a significant expression of compassion for those who receive the assistance.

Keeping Score

Which search engine did you use?

If you have a favorite charity, did you use GoodSearch.org to generate donations to their cause?

> *"We learned about dignity and decency -*
> *that how hard you work matters more than*
> *how much you make... that helping others*
> *means more than just getting ahead*
> *yourself."*
> *- Michelle Obama*
> *First Lady, United States of America*
> *Lawyer*

DAY 3: ACKNOWLEDGE SOMEONE YOU KNOW

*"Don't leave inferences to be drawn when
evidence can be presented."*
- Richard Wright
Author

Today's Adventure

Tell someone you know what you love, respect or admire about them.

Compassion in Action

Speaking the acknowledgement is the second part of today's challenge. The first part is taking a moment to conscientiously discover what you love and enjoy about the people in your life. It may be what they do, how they do it or a way that they are with others. It's entirely permissible to think about possible compliments before you speak. You can even think them over before you leave the house if that makes it any easier.

Think of three to five people you'll definitely see later today. What can you acknowledge them for based on what you already know about them? How can you say it in a way that helps them see who they are, what they do or how they do it as a gift? Whether you speak complimentary words to these individuals or others, you'll make their day.

"Nice shoes!" is a compliment. So is, "You always wear really nice shoes." But a soul validating version is to say "I've never met anyone who can pull together a beautiful ensemble as seemingly effortless as you. There is a talented artist inside you that shows up in the way you dress." Now, that's creating the experience of love with words.

Mastering Compassion

Compliment someone who normally irritates or annoys you. If you don't experience anyone as irritating or annoying, compliment someone whom you find unappealing in even the slightest way for any reason.

Keeping Score

Who did you acknowledge?

What did you acknowledge?

If you did not acknowledge anyone, what got in the way?

"There are two ways of exerting one's strength: one is pushing down, the other is pulling up."
- Booker T. Washington
Educator, Author, Orator

DAY 4: GIVE YOUR CHANGE TO CHARITY

"Now we're in the midst of not just
advocating for change, not just calling for
change - we're doing the grinding,
sometimes frustrating work of delivering
change - inch by inch, day by day."
- Barack Obama
President of the United States of America
Nobel Peace Prize, 2009

Today's Action

Change for change.

Compassion in Action

The world can't wait for each of us to have a spare million dollars to invest in a better world. A little change from each of us makes a difference to the people and charities who receive it.

Use a jar, a can or any hollowed knick-knack to collect found pennies and your own spare change. At the end of each day, drop in your pennies and extra change. At the end of the month, give it away.

Go ahead, pick up the abandoned change others leave behind at entrances, exits, food stands and so on. This is change for your charity. You know it all adds up. Whether you collect ninety cents or nine dollars, the money is a meaningful contribution to the charity of your choice. At the end of the month, roll your coins or use a coin-to-currency machine in your local grocery or bank lobby. According to Coinstar, "If half of Americans living within two miles of a Coinstar® machine donated just $1 in spare change to the American Red Cross, it would raise more than $65 million to support American Red Cross lifesaving services in communities nationwide."

While Coinstar charges a processing fee to convert your change to currency, they charge a smaller fee if you elect to donate your coins directly to a charity. Audubon Society, Feeding America, UNICEF and World Wildlife Fund are among several charities to choose from at the time you drop in your coins.

Or, eliminate the fee entirely by selecting a gift card in lieu of cash. Charity doesn't have to go through a large organization to make a meaningful difference. Any school, public or private, elementary or high school can find a way to use an Amazon.com gift card. What if they ordered a copy of this eBook for their entire student body? Just a thought.

Want other options? Visit the Audubon Society's PenniesForThePlanet.com and discover how your pennies can help the planet. If you have children, visit CommonCents.org and share the power of giving pennies with your children.

Mastering Compassion

Ask your family, friends, coworkers and acquaintances for their pennies or change to increase the impact. Tell them why you're asking and invite them to join you.

Keeping Score

How much change did you put aside for charity today?

Did you ask anyone for their change or make an effort to look for spare change in the usual and unusual places?

If you did not collect change today, why not?

"Hearts are the strongest when they beat in response to noble ideals."
- Ralph J. Bunche
Diplomat, Nobel Peace Prize, 1950

Need Help Selecting a Worthy Charity?

Visit ShyneEveryDay.com and click on "Choosing a Charity to Support."

DAY 5: LISTEN TO SOMEONE

"You've got to find some way of saying it
without saying it."
- Duke Ellington
Composer, Conductor, Pianist

Today's Adventure

Listen to someone. Really listen.

Compassion in Action

Anyone who offers their ears without adding their lips is extending compassion. Something incredible happens when we are truly heard. We may not say anything to the hearer, but we know the difference between being listened to and being humored or tolerated.

Someone says, "Can I talk to you? There's something on my mind." The other person says, "Yeah, sure." Oftentimes, sooner than later, the listener becomes the talker. Unsolicited advice flows freely. Empathetic stories creep in and then take over the conversation. Even when the listener does not advise or share their similar tales, judgments on the legitimacy of the speaker's concern dictates the response.

Listening is an act of discipline. Far from passive, the silence of listening is a miraculous act of compassion.

We're powerful beings. Smart, too. When we speak our concerns aloud, we hear ourselves. Our frustration dissipates. Our options become apparent. We solve our own problems when we can see them. Somehow, seeing through someone else's ears adds clarity.

Mastering Compassion

Call someone with whom you can predict every miserable, predictable turn in the conversation. And instead of saying the usual responses, just listen. If you usually give advice, don't. If in the past you've tried to explain something to them, just for today, fuhgettaboutit. Grant them fresh ears.

Keeping Score

To whom did you listen today?

If you did not listen to someone, what got in the way?

"To talk to someone who does not listen is enough to tense the devil."
– Pearl Bailey
Actress, Singer

DAY 6: CLEAN SOMETHING

*"Don't sit down and wait for the
opportunities to come; you have to get up
and make them."*
- Madame C. J. Walker
Entrepreneur, Philanthropist.

Today's Adventure

Clean something that doesn't belong to you.

Compassion in Action

Pick up a single piece of trash off the street. Clean
something at your place of work that it is not your job to
clean. Wipe down the counter in a public restroom. Of
course, only do this if it does not cause you to violate
anyone else's sense of privacy and personal space.
Definitely, only do so if it will not break any laws or
established rules. Notice any resistance to cleaning up
other people's messes. It may not be your mess, but it is
your environment. Whose world is it, if it isn't yours?

Mastering Compassion

As you go through your day, notice any litter on the
sidewalk, around trash cans, in parks, etc. Pick up five
pieces of litter, trash, recyclables or other discarded
items. Do this in addition to cleaning something that
doesn't belong to you.

Keeping Score

Where and what did you clean?

If you did not complete today's act of compassion, what got in the way?

> *"A life is not important except in the*
> *impact it has on other lives."*
> *- Jackie Robinson*
> *Professional Baseball Player,*
> *National League MVP, 1949*

DAY 7: SMILE

*"I have the smile and charisma of my
mother and the big heart of my mom,
because she wants to save the world and
help the world, so I am just like her."*
— *Magic Johnson*
*Entrepreneur, Dream Team Athlete, LA
Lakers*

Today's Adventure

Share your smile with five people you normally might
not.

Compassion in Action

Whether we realize it or not, we develop smile
guidelines. We smile at people we know. We smile at
people who are "safe". We smile in pleasant public
situations. We smile when we think it will get us better
service. And, certainly, when it might yield a discount or
benefit. On the other side, we don't smile at people in
certain occupations. We don't smile at people of a certain
class. We don't smile at people of a certain age. And we
definitely don't smile if we can tell from looking at them
that they are not going to perform the honor of smiling
back.

Just as compassion is a habit so is fear and resignation.
Afraid of the unknown, we let concern over how our

smile will be received prevent us from lighting up someone's day.

Smiling at your parents, kids or the coworkers you hang out with regularly is not the type of stretch that makes this an adventure. As you go through the day, notice your smile guidelines. Then go beyond them. Smile.

Mastering Compassion

Every time you think about smiling at someone and hear that little voice give you a reason not to do it, do it anyway.

Keeping Score

Did you complete today's action?

If you did, describe what happened.

What was it like for you? If you did not complete it, what got in the way?

> *"When I look out at the people and they look at me and they're smiling, then I know I'm loved."*
> *— Etta James*
> *Singer, Songwriter*

DAY 8 GIVE AWAY ONE DOLLAR

"That which could hunger, could starve."
- Octavia Butler
Author, Science Fiction

Today's Adventure

Give away one dollar.

Compassion in Action

It's up to you whether you choose someone who is requesting money or to do so on a whim. If you live or work in an area populated with panhandlers or representatives of charities requesting donations at places of business, this will be a little easier to do. To count, you have to actually hand the person your dollar, getting nothing in return. No chocolate bars, no extra foam on your latte. Notice the number of people you come across in a day who could use your dollar.

This isn't about the amount of money you give. If you're tempted to make it five or ten or one hundred dollars, that's something different. You can do that, too. But on one occasion give away exactly one dollar and notice how many people you come across in a day that can use a single dollar. If you're rich, it's humbling. If you're struggling, it's still humbling.

If you have any concern that giving away money devalues the receiver or the possibility that your dollar will support a poor life choice, let it go. Complete the day's act of compassion and leave the rest to a higher power to manage.

Mastering Compassion

Go online and give ten minutes to donate sponsors money to those in need at no cost to you. FreeRice.com donates free rice to the hungry in rich and poor nations. For each correct answer to vocabulary, math, geography, science or a few other subjects, they donate ten grains of rice. Ten minutes could result in a donation of a cup of rice. That won't end hunger, but it does help you appreciate that our many ways to help those in need besides writing a check from your own account. Other websites that contribute someone else's resources to good causes are Charitii.org, thenoprofits.com and care2.org.

Keeping Score

To whom did you give your dollar?

Why that person?

What did you notice about the level of basic or financial need in your community?

If you did not complete it, what got in the way?

"Every dollar that is printed should not represent a debt to private bankers. It should represent an investment potential in the common good in the common needs of our country."
— Cynthia McKinney
Politician, Activist

DAY 9   THANK THOSE WHO SERVE

*"In recognizing the humanity of our fellow
beings, we pay ourselves the highest
tribute."*
- Thurgood Marshall
Supreme Court Justice, 1967-1991

Today's Action

Find out who represents you and thank them for their
service.

Compassion in Action

Many of our esteemed African-American heroes and
heroines bettered our lives by working with or as elected
representatives. Use SearchKindly.org, Ecosearch.org or
LookPink.com to find out the names of your city council
representative; state legislative representatives; and your
three national law-making representatives. If you're in
the United States, you are represented by a member of the
House of Representatives and two Senators. You're just a
click or two away from finding out who's representing
your interests.

After you jot down their names, visit the webpage of at
least one of these individuals to see what they've done for
you lately.

Whether or not you agree with everything they've done
or their political party, let them know you recognize that

they are doing the best they can. If you're so inclined, share your views on an issue that is important to you.

If you think they deserve to stay in office, consider a donation. Even a single dollar sends a message.

Many of the leaders used their voice to champion compassion. In a democracy, your vote is your voice. Need to register? Visit registertovote.org.

Mastering Compassion

In most national elections, less than forty percent of Americans cast a vote for their House of Representatives member. Even fewer write or email them about an issue of importance to them.

After visiting their sites, contact at least one of your elected law-making representatives to express your view on an issue of importance to you. Because so few Americans contact their representatives, they know each letter often represents the unexpressed views of hundreds.

> *"Nobody's free until everybody's free."*
> *– Fannie Lou Hamer*
> *Civil Rights Activist*

DAY 10   EXPRESS THANKS

*"Thank you is the best prayer that anyone
could say. I say that one a lot. Thank you
expresses extreme gratitude, humility,
understanding."*
— Alice Walker
Author

Today's Adventure

Write a thank you note and actually send it.

Compassion in Action

It doesn't matter for what. It can be for something recent or something someone did long ago. Don't worry about how much time has passed. Thank you notes are never too late. Don't worry about sloppy handwriting, poor grammar, your style, or the format you choose. Only think about the value of letting someone know the difference they made.

Mastering Compassion

Send two.

Keeping Score

Who did you thank?

What was it like for you?

If you did not complete it, what got in the way?

*"We must express ourselves in ways that
demonstrate our respect for others."
- Stephen Carter
Law Professor, Author*

DAY 11   ACKNOWLEDGE A STRANGER

"Invest in the human soul. Who knows, it
might be a diamond in the rough."
– Mary McLeod Bethune
Educator, Activist

Today's Adventure

Compliment a stranger.

Compassion in Action

Just like Day 2's acknowledgement of someone you knew, say it in a way that helps them see who they are, what they do or how they do it as a gift? If you are someone who does this easily, compliment five strangers.

Mastering Compassion

As you go throughout your day, notice the times you consider smiling at someone and choose not to do so. Ask yourself what it was about them that turned you off. Or, said a different way, what was your thought about them that took away your willingness to smile at will?

Keeping Score

Who did you acknowledge?

What was about them that inspired you to acknowledge them as opposed to all the other people you could have acknowledged?

Which acknowledgement do you hear the most?

Which acknowledgements are you most likely to give others?

If you did not complete it, what got in the way?

"Find the good. It's all around you. Find it, showcase it and you'll start believing in it."
- Jesse Owens
Olympic Athlete

DAY 12   GIVE AWAY A BOOK, MUSIC OR ART

*"Science provides an understanding of a
universal experience. Arts provide a
universal understanding of a personal
experience."*
– Mae Jemison
Astronaut, Researcher, Entrepreneur

Today's Adventure

Give away a book.

Compassion in Action

Choose a book that really made a difference in your life. The book is symbolic of the true gift. You took the time to consider who among your friends, family or acquaintances might truly appreciate it. If, after thinking of everyone you know, you can't imagine a single person who'd be interested, then drop it off at a school, shelter or used bookstore with a wish that it lands in the right person's hands. If you don't have any books to share, substitute a different artistic expression that has inspired you. A unique compilation of music on CD might work.

Although it will be awesome if the person actually reads the book, plays the music or otherwise enjoys your gift, that's not your concern today. Today is about you being a contribution to another. If they read it, play it or enjoy it and tell you about it, then that is their gift of love to you.

Separate giving from your expectations of how it ought to be received or used.

Mastering Compassion

Find one other item of any type to give away. It can be another book or CD. Or, something else that its recipient will be able to use, appreciate or enjoy.

Keeping Score

Which book, CD or other item did you give away?

Why did you choose that item?

What is it you hope the gift provides the recipient?

If you did not complete today's act of compassion, what got in the way?

> *"My Alma Mater was books, a good library...I could spend the rest of my life reading, just satisfying my curiosity."*
> *– Malcolm X*
> *Civil Rights Activist*

Day 13   Share A Talent

"A good deed here, a good deed there, a good thought here, a good comment there, all added up to my career in one way or another."
- Sidney Poitier
Actor, Author, Director, Diplomat
Academy Award Winner, 1963

Today's Adventure

Share one of your talents.

Compassion in Action

This can look about seven and half billion different ways. If you're a musician, surprise someone with a song. Do you cook? Make a special meal for a friend, a shut-in, a neighbor, a colleague or a whole group of folks. Not an artsy person? Mr. Fixit, fix something. Ms. Organized, organize something for someone.

It's up to you how much time you dedicate to completing today's act of compassion. All of us have multiple gifts. Choose to share the one that your day's schedule allows you to share comfortably to keep the spirit of fun and ease in the game. However, if you can go all out, don't hold back.

If you're at a complete loss, scroll back through numbers 1 through 11 and do the one you enjoyed the most.

Mastering Compassion

Locate a charity that can use your talent and schedule a time to volunteer within the next thirty days.

Keeping Score

Which talent did you share?]

With whom did you share it?

What was it like to share that talent with that person?

If you did not complete today's act of compassion, what got in the way?

> *"Nothing great or enduring, especially in music, has ever sprung full-fledged and unprecedented from the brain of any master; the best he gives to the world he gathers from the hearts of the people, and runs it through the alembic of his genius."*
> *- James Weldon Johnson*
> *Lawyer, Diplomat, Educator, Author*
> *Songwriter, Poet*
> *"Lift Every Voice and Sing"*

Day 14   Donate Something To Charity

"Happiness doesn't result from what we
get, but from what we give."
– Ben Carson
Heart Surgeon

Today's Adventure

Donate Something.

Compassion in Action

There's something you have and don't want that someone else doesn't have and does want. Even if it's a want they don't yet know they have. There's a thrift store, charity or shelter that will benefit from your donation.

If there's something in your closet that looks practically new but you haven't worn or used it in over a year, there's a good chance it's time has passed for you. If you haven't used or worn it in three years and it still looks good…give it away and clear a space for something new to come to you.

Got an old pair of sneaker in a corner, under a bed or behind the new ones? Nike sponsors the Reuse A Shoe program which turns worn out gym shoes into safer surfaces for playgrounds and athletic facilities. Old eyeglasses can be donated at many major eyewear stores and private practitioners. Check out OneSight.org (find drop-off locations.) or New-Eyes.org . Give an old pair of still wearable jeans to TeensForJeans through DoSomething.org. They'll get them to homeless teenagers. Don't be thrown off by Teens For Jeans' connection to Aeropostale. They accept jeans of any and all brands and sizes as long as they are in good condition.

Mastering Compassion

Most of us have more than a single item that is sitting in the house unused and unlikely to ever be used. If you can spare a few extra minutes, donate several items that another can use.

Keeping Score

What did you give away and to whom?

For how long had you considered giving this item away, if this applies?

How did it feel to donate that item or give it away?

If you did not complete today's act of compassion, what got in the way?

"From what we get, we can make a living;
what we give, however, makes a life."
– Arthur Ashe
Professional Tennis Player
Won Triple Grand Slams

DAY 15   EXPRESS YOUR GRATITUDE

*"No matter what accomplishments you
make, somebody helps you."*
− Wilma Rudolph
Olympic Athlete

Today's Adventure

Express your gratitude.

Compassion in Action

Think of five things you're glad you have and tell someone about it. Whether you have tons of material possessions or a handful, there is so much to be grateful for on any given day. If you're reading this, you are still alive. Today is an opportunity. Two things to be grateful for before we even get to friends, family or material resources.

Are there people in your life that make a difference? Which of their talents, gifts, abilities or experiences add value to your life? Tell them.

Mastering Compassion

Tell five different people five things you're grateful for without telling them it is a part of this assignment. Notice what it inspires in them.

Keeping Score

What are five to ten things you are grateful for today?

What was it like to share your gratitude with others?

How did they respond?

If you did not complete today's act of compassion, what got in the way?

"Speech is a very important aspect of being human. A whisper doesn't cut it."
– James Earl Jones
Actor, Academy Award winner; multiple Emmy, Screen Actors and Golden Globe awards.

DAY 16   WATCH YOUR WORDS

*"If the word has the potency to revive and
make us free, it has also the power to
blind, imprison, and destroy."*
– Ralph Ellison
Scholar, Novelist, Literary Critic

Today's Adventure

Pay attention to how you use our greatest technology, words. Use words intentionally.

Compassion in Action

Our words can create love in an instant. They can also create upset and dis-ease. When you recognize the power of your speaking, moment-by-moment, you begin to recognize how much your words create your experience and your world. How often do you talk about problems, worries or other people as problems? How often do you repeat meaningless phrases or clichés in place of an authentic conversation?

Avoid asking superfluous questions. Only ask how someone is doing if you intend to listen attentively to their response. Avoid using offensive words.

Minding your words today is an act of compassion toward everyone you are around today. Using your words intentionally carries with it the power to heal others.

Mastering Compassion

In addition to the above, refrain from sarcasm, teasing and gossip throughout the day.

Keeping Score

Was any part of speaking intentionally harder for you than another?

How was your day different from most other days?

If you did not complete today's act of compassion, what got in the way?

> *"A little less complaint and whining, and*
> *a little more dogged work and manly*
> *striving, would do us more credit than a*
> *thousand civil rights bills."*
> *- Dr. W. E. B. Du Bois*
> *Historian, Sociologist, Activist*
> *First African-American to receive a Ph.D.*
> *from Harvard University*

DAY 17   LOVE YOU

*"The river is constantly turning and
bending and you never know where it's
going to go and where you'll wind up.
Following the bend in the river and
staying on your own path means that you
are on the right track. Don't let anyone
deter you from that."*
- Eartha Kitt
Singer, Actress

Today's Adventure

Do something just for you.

Compassion in Action

You're doing great! You're halfway through 30 days of love. Treat yourself. This is a gift of time.

Watch a sunset. Listen to your favorite music. Take a stroll. Write in your journal. Write yourself a letter of appreciation or congratulation. Take a nap. Indulge in a bubble bath. There's something special about you. There's a reason you exist. A difference you make being the unique combination of traits that you are.

It is definitely more difficult to be compassionate with others if we neglect compassionate action toward ourselves. If you never feel worthy of a break, how can you cut someone else a break?

Take responsibility for your own daily joy. That act affirms to yourself and the universe that you know your unique value.

Mastering Compassion

Do something for yourself today that you've been putting off, avoiding or waiting to find the time. Don't settle. How can you value the dreams and desires of others, if you deny the value of your own?

Keeping Score

What did you do just for you today?

What was it like for you?

If you did not complete today's act of compassion, what got in the way?

"Breathe. Let go. And remind yourself that this very moment is the only one you know you have for sure."
– Oprah Winfrey
Media Entrepreneur, Philanthropist

DAY 18   GIVE 10 MINUTES

"Service to others is the rent you pay for
your room here on earth."
— Muhammad Ali
Heavyweight Boxing Champion

Today's Adventure

Give away 10 minutes of your time.

Compassion in Action

There are lots of options with this one. Whether you have a busy schedule from daybreak to bedtime or stroll through your day with little on your calendar, the conscious act of giving 10 minutes to assist someone or something else is compassion in action. Ask someone how they're doing and do so with genuine curiosity. Look around and notice if there's someone at work, in your home or on the street who could use a helping hand to finish something, start something or move something. Don't be shy. And don't worry about starting something you can't finish. Choose something in which ten minutes will make a difference, big or small.

Mastering Compassion

Find a way to give a full thirty minutes to someone else. Help them with a project that is important to them. If there is no one around you working on any type of project at home, work, church or play, you'll need to be creative. Is there a business establishment or local not-for-profit organization that you've thought of offering to help in some way? Today's the day.

Keeping Score

What did you do and for whom?

How did the person respond?

If you did not complete today's act of compassion, what got in the way?

"Memories of our lives, of our works and
our deeds will continue in others."
- Rosa Parks
Civil Rights Activist

Day 19 Say "I Love You."

"Let us banish fear."
– Carter G. Woodson
Historian, Author
Founder of Black History Week

Today's Adventure

Say "I love you" to someone you normally do not.

Compassion in Action

This might be your significant other or a parent or a sibling. It could be a close friend. If "I love you" flows off your lips like a river to the sea, it may take a few moments to think of someone whom you do love but to whom you do not express it aloud in three simple words.

Mastering Compassion

In addition to telling the person "I love you," include the details of what it is about them that inspires in you the awareness of valuing their unique contribution to your life and the world.

Keeping Score

To whom did you say "I love you"?

Search your relationships. Name three people who don't hear "I love you" very often.

If you did not complete today's act of compassion, what got in the way?

"Love makes your soul crawl out from its
hiding place."
– Zora Neale Hurston
Author

DAY 20 PLAY ONLINE GAMES, GENERATE DONATIONS

"In a sane, civil, intelligent and moral society, you don't blame poor people for being poor."
- Andrew Young
Mayor, Congressman, Ambassador

Today's Action

Go online and answer short, simple questions to generate resources for others.

Compassion in Action

Several sites allow players to "win" money for charity. FreeRice.com and Charitii.com are two good options. These sites test your knowledge of words or facts. Each game automatically adjusts the level of difficulty to stay engaging but not annoyingly difficulty. The sites want you to win for charity and have fun doing it. They want you to come back.

FreeRice.com is among the most well-known. When you click on the page, you land on the basic word game. Match up the correct meaning to the word shown and it generates a donation from sponsors and partners. Each correct response translates to a donation of ten grains of rice. It's quick and there are multiple levels to keep you challenged. Go to the site, answer ten questions correctly and you've donated 100 grains of rice.

If words aren't your favorite topic, click on "Subjects". FreeRice.com covers the sciences, humanities, geography, math, languages and SAT test prep. Use the languages option to learn basic words in Spanish, French, Italian, Latin or German while donating. It's easy. It's free. It's charity.

Charitii.org is a word game, crossword-clue style. As your skill increases, so does the number of letters they drop from the answer choices. Unlike FreeRice.com, this site lets you choose from several different charities including The Nature Conservancy and the Invisible Youth Network.

You won't single-handedly alleviate world hunger in an hour by playing a game. However, if you play periodically while waiting for downloads, between tasks or in place of playing the latest, greatest social media crush, you can generate a donation large enough to feed a family every month.

Need a reason to make playing games for charity a habit? Doctors agree that keeping the mind active helps prevent the decline of our mental functioning as we age. If you're a little older than the internet, it can't hurt to challenge the mind each day while giving away other peoples' money.

Mastering Compassion

Use FreeRice.com and don't stop until you've donated a cup of rice, about 7000 grains. Do it in one or several sittings. Also, consider setting up an account on either or both sites to tabulate your impact at the end of the game.

Both let you log on with your Facebook account. Posting your latest donation could inspire your connections.

Keeping Score

Which game did you play?

How much did you generate for charity?

> *"There are many persons ready to do what is right because in their hearts they know it is right. But they hesitate, waiting for the other fellow to make the make the first move - and he, in turn, waits for you."*
> *- Marian Anderson*
> *Singer, First African-American to perform at the Metropolitan Opera in New York, NY (1955)*

DAY 21   DO SOMETHING FOR THE PLANET

"The earth we share is not just a rock
tossed through space, but a living,
nurturing being. She cares for us. She
deserves our care in return."
– Michael Jackson
Musical Genius, Philanthropist

Today's Adventure

Do something for the planet.

Compassion in Action

Recycle something you normally do not. If you're not an avid recycler, this will be easy. Instead of putting that bottle, can or paper in the trash, find a place to recycle it. If you have an old phone or other electronic device, use the internet to find a nearby drop-off location.

Composting trash will grow your garden greener. Prefer cash? Give $5 to a charity that plants trees, conserves nature or protects habitats and species. The Canopy Project is part of The Earth Day Network and highly recommended. It may not be your mess, but it is your environment.

Looking for something you can do from your computer or mobile device? Replace your current search browser with   http://ecosearch.org,   http://searchkindly.org   or http://goodsearch.com to donate to charities each time you search. Your searches will help save the planet. Also, check out http://ecologyfund.com. You click and sponsors donate to earth-preserving charities.

Recycle your old cell phone, laptop or other e-waste. Finding a recycling site is easier than ever. Visit Earth911.org, Call2Recycle.org, or GreenerGadgets.org. On Earth911.org, go to the top, right of the navigation bar on the home page. Click on recycling search. Enter your item and your location and they'll tell you a nearby place to drop it off. At GreenerGadget.org, enter your zip right on the home page to find a nearby recycling location. Call2Recycle.org is specifically for finding locations that accept cell phones and rechargeable batteries. The average American purchases a new cell every 18-24 months. Where are all the old ones?

Mastering Compassion

Discover and take on one new habit that supports the earth.

Keeping Score

What did you do for planet earth today?

"You're either part of the solution or
you're part of the problem."
– Eldridge Cleaver
Writer, Activist

Day 22   Compassionate Touch Heals

"Why is it that, as a culture, we are more
comfortable seeing two men holding guns
than holding hands?"
— Ernest Gaines
Author

Today's Adventure

Hug a loved one today.

Compassion in Action

If you are not a hugger or hugging is not part of your relationship with a parent, sibling or friend, today's the day to hug. Holding hands works, too.

While walking my dog in the park one day, I noticed two young girls, probably seven- or eight-years-old. They skipped across the grass holding hands en route to the play area. It stood out to me. In American society, we don't expect to see friends holding hands past childhood. Even couples sometimes limit holding hands to date nights.

We are physical beings. Physical touch has the capacity to heal. Search the web and you will find that many a study confirms that touch is powerful medicine. When a parent kisses their child's "boo-boo" it is helping the healing process.

- Put your arm around a loved one's shoulder.
- Hug a parent, child, spouse, friend or relative.
- Hold hands while you walk with friend, child, spouse or relative.

If you'll only see coworkers and acquaintances today, weigh whether a pat on the back for a job well done is an appropriate option.

Find a way to connect physically with your environment if there is absolutely no way for you to appropriately connect with another person. Hug a tree. Lie in the grass. Roll around in the snow.

Mastering Compassion

As you go through the day, notice individuals who may not enjoy the luxury of human touch on a regular basis. It is enough just to engage in noticing. If you are especially empathetic, this exercise may be emotionally taxing. Only if you are moved to do so, ask one of them if you can offer them a hug.

Keeping Score

Describe today's act of compassion?

If you did not complete today's act of compassion, what got in the way?

> *"Love is that condition in the human spirit*
> *so profound that it allows me to survive,*
> *and better than that, to thrive with*
> *passion, compassion and style."*
> *- Maya Angelou*
> *Poet, Author*

DAY 23   MAKE A REQUEST

"Some say we are responsible for those
we love. Others know we are responsible
for those who love us."
– Nikki Giovanni
Poet, Activist, Educator

Today's Adventure

Ask someone for something.

Compassion in Action

Give the gift of contribution. Let someone do something for you. Almost all of us know someone who loves to do stuff for us. Trouble is we don't always want what they wish to contribute to us. It may be a child who wants to fix-up our hair, but we're too busy. Ask them for a makeover. If your spouse makes too much of a mess when they do that thing they love to do for you, today, ask them to do it for you anyway.

And, of course, thank them afterwards.

Mastering Compassion

Ask a relative to do something for you. Your mother would love this one. If there's a relative that is always asking you for a favor, ask them for something that it is within their power to do for you. The gift is asking, not receiving. However, receiving their response is another act of compassion.

Keeping Score

Whom did you allow to contribute to you and in what way?

How did they respond to your request?

If you did not complete today's act of compassion, what got in the way?

> *"I have this ability to find this hidden talent in people that sometimes even they didn't know they had."*
> *- Berry Gordy*
> *Founder, Motown Record Corporation*
> *Songwriter, Producer*

DAY 24 LET LAUGHTER HEAL

*"Like a welcome summer rain, humor may
suddenly cleanse and cool the earth, the
air and you."*
– Langston Hughes
Poet

Today's Adventure

Make someone laugh.

Compassion in Action

Laughter heals. It releases pent up, stale energy. That makes laughter an act of compassion.

Know a good joke? Know a bad one? Ever notice that the silliest jokes sometimes get the biggest laughs. Jokes told incorrectly can work too. A woman at work who was nearing retirement started telling a joke about the three good things that come from having Alzheimer's. She stated the first two and when she got to the third, stumbled a bit and finally said, "Oh darn, I can't remember the last one." We all laughed. Turned out there was a real third benefit that completed the joke, but her new version is the joke we retell.

If jokes aren't your thing, try a funny face. Kids love them. Young kids love them. Those going through the teenage years are more likely to scowl at a funny face than laugh, but their hearts are touched just the same.

Costumes, funny hats or a YouTube comedy scene shared, all work.

Mastering Compassion

Surf the web and find a new joke to make your own. Share it more than once.

Keeping Score

Who did you make laugh and how?

How much fun did you have with today's small act of compassion?

If you did not complete today's act of compassion, what got in the way?

> *"And tired" always followed sick. Worst beating I ever got in my life, my mother said, "I am just sick..." And I said, "And tired." I don't remember anything after that."*
> *– Bill Cosby*
> *Comedian*

DAY 25   FORGIVE SOMEONE

"As an artist I come to sing, but as a
citizen, I will always speak for peace, and
no one can silence me in this."
- Paul Robeson
Singer, Writer, Activist

Today's Adventure

Forgive someone.

Compassion in Action

If forgiveness were easy, there wouldn't be enough books written on it to fill a small bookstore. Religions, twelve step programs and healing arts all acknowledge the power of forgiveness to transform our life. If you're ready to forgive big, do it. Otherwise, we can keep it simple.

Think of an action someone took that still bothers you to do this day—a remark, an omission, an inconsideration. Now, here's the shortcut to accessing the spirit of forgiveness. Think of a time when you did something similar to someone else, intentionally or not. Take a moment to look carefully until you find a situation that allows you to relate to them. Why did you do it? How did it affect the other person? What would life be like if everyone who met you was told that story about you and nothing else? Extending forgiveness expands the heart.

Mastering Compassion

If you haven't apologized for a grievance someone holds against you, do that today also. If there is no way to reach this person because they are no longer living or relocated to someplace unknown to you, apologize aloud as if they can hear you or write it out in a letter. If you write the letter, I recommend destroying it afterward as an act of accepting your own forgiveness by letting it go.

Keeping Score

Whom did you forgive today and for what past act?

How did you feel afterwards?

If you did not complete today's act of compassion, what got in the way?

> *"How far you go in life depends on your*
> *being tender with the young,*
> *compassionate with the aged, sympathetic*
> *with the striving and tolerant of the weak*
> *and strong. Because someday in your life*
> *you will have been all of these."*
> *- George Washington Carver*
> *Scientist, Inventor, Educator*

DAY 26   GIVE SOMETHING TO SOMEONE

*"I always wanted to be somebody. If I
made it, it's half because I was game
enough to take a lot of punishment along
the way and half because there were a lot
of people who cared enough to help me."*
- Althea Gibson,
Professional Athlete
Wimbledon Winner, 1956, 1957, 1958

Today's Adventure

Give something away.

Compassion in Action

There's something you have and don't want that someone else doesn't have and does want. Even if it's a want they don't yet know they have.

Before you search for the nearest thrift store, take a moment to find out if you have something to offer someone you know.

> *Examples:*
> **A friend complimented you on a scarf that you don't often wear. Gift it to her.*
> **A child loves to play with something of yours that is collecting dust except for when he plays with it. Assuming it isn't a safety hazard for the child's age, gift it.*

A coworker loves a desktop knick-knack that isn't particularly sentimental to you. Gift it.
A neighbor constantly comments about a garden decoration. Gift it.

If it is too awkward for you to give it away today or impossible because you won't see the people who come to mind, then, by all means, drop something off at a local thrift store, shelter or other appropriate location.

Just like Day 14, anything in your closet that looks practically new but hasn't seen light in over a year is a place to start. Give it away and clear a space for something new to come to you.

Mastering Compassion

Give away something that you've been holding onto for all the wrong reasons. Is there something left over from a long ago relationship that is anchoring you to the past? Is there an item you've outgrown, but you are hanging onto it as a symbol of glory days gone by? Put the past where it belongs and seek out today's gift, today's love, today's glory.

Keeping Score

What did you give away?

What was it like for you?

If you did not complete today's act of compassion, what got in the way?

"Being considerate of others will take you and your children further in life than any college or professional degree."
— Marianne Wright Edelman
Philanthropist,
Founder and President,
Children's Defense Fund

DAY 27 CALCULATE YOUR GLOBAL FOOTPRINT

"I am, was, and always will be a catalyst
for change."
— Shirley Chisholm
Congressperson, House of Representatives
Presidential Candidate, 1972

Today's Action

Use the internet to calculate your global footprint.

Compassion in Action

A little information goes a long way in making informed choices. How can you appreciate the importance of reducing, reusing and recycling if you don't know the effect of your current lifestyle on natural resources and on the planet as a whole? Compassion for our planet begins with awareness of our impact.

FootprintNetwork.org is one of several websites that calculates your global footprint. It walks you through about ten different lifestyle questions. They even use catchy animation to demonstrate the impact of your choices. After the final question, it measures the impact of your lifestyle on the planet, your global footprint. This is the same calculator used on the Earth Day Network site.

MyFootprint.org offers a more comprehensive review of your lifestyle choices by asking more specific questions in a multiple choice format. MichaelBlueJay.com's carbon footprint calculator allows you to compare your household footprint with that of the typical American household.

By measuring your global footprint, the impact of your lifestyle and choices on the planet, you gain insight into the importance of your day-to-day choices. If you've calculated your footprint recently, complete today's "Mastering Compassion" action.

Mastering Compassion

Calculate your global footprint on two different sites and commit to one new action that will reduce your global footprint.

Keeping Score

What most surprised you after calculating your global footprint?

Name one habit you'd be willing to change today to lessen the carbon footprint you leave behind.

"There is no such thing as making the miracle happen spontaneously and on the spot. You've got to work."
- Martina Arroyo
Opera Singer

DAY 28 CREATE A BETTER WORLD

"I believe in prayer. It's the best way we
have to draw strength from heaven."
— Josephine Baker
Dancer, Singer, Actress

Today's Action

Pray for a world at peace and a world in harmony.

Compassion in Action

Do this for ten minutes. Ten minutes can seem longer than you think, so consider breaking it up into peace in your community, in your city, in your state, in your nation and in the world for 2 minutes each.

Or visit the World Peace Prayer Society or Fellowship of Reconciliation. Examples of prayer for peace can be found at 2HeartsNetwork.org.

If you don't believe in prayer, imagine the world surrounded by love or light. If neither prayer nor imagining work for you, find one new way to support peace or harmony and do it. That may mean writing a letter to a world leader or signing an online petition.

Mastering Compassion

Pray, imagine or meditate on world peace for five minutes every day for one week. It doesn't seem like a lot, but if you previously spent zero time each day contemplating a world at peace, the exercise in compassion will grow your soul.

If 10,000 people did this, it changes what's possible because it makes peace and harmony a bit more plausible to 10,000 powerful, creative human beings.

Keeping Score

How did you promote world peace?

Can you commit to the Mastering Compassion exercise for one week?

"The Lord was pleased to strengthen us,
and remove all fear from us, and disposed
our hearts to be as useful as possible."
- Richard Allen
Minister, Abolitionist, Activist

DAY 29 REPEAT YOUR FAVORITE COMPASSIONATE ACT

"I've missed more than 9000 shots in my career. I've lost almost 300 games. 26 times, I've been trusted to take the game winning shot and missed. I've failed over and over and over again in my life. And that is why I succeed."
– Michael Jordan

Today's Adventure

Pick your favorite day. Now go big!

Compassion in Action

Pretend that a chorus of angels has been watching you throughout the month. Sometimes they helped, sometimes they challenged you. Now they applaud your February 2014 Adventure in Compassion.

What is your encore? Somewhere along the way, an act of compassion occurred to you that seemed too ridiculous to tackle. Perhaps today is the day to put all concern aside and go for it.

If nothing else comes to mind, share yourself. Share a story of a particular day's love and surprise. Share what was harder than you expected about making love every day. Share what was easier than you anticipated. Share why you chose to challenge yourself in the first place.

Mastering Compassion

Share the impact of completing the Adventures in Compassion with five people you care about. Recommend they grow their heart and soul in the same way you have. Encourage them to have Adventures in Compassion.

Keeping Score

How did you finish off the month?

With which five people did you share your Adventures in Compassion?

If you haven't told them about it, I trust you're not waiting for inspiration to love them with the gift of recommending an Adventure in Compassion.

"But at the same time you can't assume that making a difference 20 years ago is going to allow you to sort of live on the laurels of those victories for the rest of your life."
- Angela Davis
Scholar, Activist

DAY 30 INSPIRE COMPASSION

"The people must know before they can
act, and there is no educator to compare
with the press."
- Ida B. Wells
Suffragist, Journalist, Civil Rights Activist

Today's Action

Call, write, post, tweet or photo-post about a cause, charity, group or event that matters to you.

Compassion in Action

By now your friends and family know you've been making a difference all month. You may have already asked them to use SearchKindly.org, give up their pennies and play FreeRice.com. Now tell them why.

What difference in the world do you hope to see in your lifetime? Is there an organization dedicated to that change? Is there a local food bank, shelter or family making a right-now difference in your community?

Invite your friends and family to invite them to care about your cause and do something.

Mastering Compassion

Ask five people to actively join a cause, charity, community group or event that matters to you. All five may say "Yes" and support it. All may say "No." You've made a difference every day for nearly a month. If you developed a new passion or affirmed an old one, give others the opportunity to join you.

> *"The tragedy of life doesn't lie in not*
> *reaching your goal. The tragedy lies in*
> *having no goal to reach."*
> *- Benjamin E. Mays*
> *Scholar, Educator, Activist*

Thank You

*"God and Nature first made us what we
are, and then out of our own created
genius we make ourselves what we want to
be. Follow always that great law. Let the
sky and God be our limit and Eternity our
measurement."*
– Marcus Garvey
Jamaican-born Activist

Thank you for celebrating the past by actively creating a better future for all of us. On behalf of those who benefited from your generous and open spirit, I thank you. Your actions made a difference to more people than you can imagine.

While completing the month of compassionate action is an end to itself, consistent with my other titles, here's a way to measure your participation.

Grand Master of Compassion – Complete all 30 acts of love as they were designed each day in the proper order. If you did this on the first go, you are incredible. You're probably a saint or perhaps an angel walking amongst us.

Master of Compassion – Complete each of the 30 tasks. If you completed all 30 acts, but occasionally doubled up after missing a day, you're still a master. "Occasionally" translates to five or fewer missed days.

Compassion Practitioner – Complete at least 25 of the 30 acts of love.

Compassion Apprentice – Complete at least 20 of the 30 acts of love.

Compassion Novice – Complete at least 15 of the 30 acts of love.

Compassion Aspirant – Complete at least 10 of the 30 acts of love.

What's next?

If you are a Grand Master of Compassion, you live and breathe compassion. Generosity is in your being.

For everyone else, you might take a few days to regroup and then start it again. Or try one of the other titles in The Compassion Series. Expect a repeat or two or five if you take the other Adventures. However, each is uniquely designed and ordered to create an impact that is distinct from the others.

If the novelty of the game has worn off but you enjoyed it all the same, consider adopting your favorite act of compassion as a daily or weekly habit as appropriate. Or make up your own unique Sunday-to-Saturday seven acts of love weekly combo plan.

Keep Love Alive

Help spread the word. When you give Adventures in Compassion a review, your reach goes beyond your immediate circle of friends, family and acquaintances. If you enjoyed the adventure and are moved to leave a five star review, it inspires others to take the leap and have an Adventure in Compassion.

This can be just another cool book of neat actions to take or it can become a movement that transforms the planet.

Life is a journey. Adventure is optional.

> *"I am not a perfect servant. I am a public servant doing my best against the odds. As I develop and serve, be patient. God is not finished with me yet."*
> *- Jesse Jackson*
> *Civil Rights Activist*
> *Presidential Candidate, 1984, 1988*

Celebrating a History of Compassion, Black History Month 2014 is part of The Compassion Series. Each book in the series is designed to improve the human condition and the world in which we live. Please visit ShyneEveryDay.com. And don't forget to post a review on Amazon.com.

Thank you.

Rahbin Shyne

"Love is patient,
love is kind.
It does not envy,
it does not boast,
it is not proud.
It does not dishonor others,
it is not self-seeking,
it is not easily angered,
it keeps no record of wrongs.
Love does not delight in evil
but rejoices with the truth.
It always protects,
always trusts,
always hopes,
always perseveres."
1 Corinthians 13:4-7